Meet a Baby Mountain Lion

Whitney Sanderson

Lerner Publications • Minneapolis

For my baby,
Faisal

Lerner Publications Company
An imprint of Lerner Publishing Group, Inc.
241 First Avenue North
Minneapolis, MN 55401 USA

For reading levels and more information, look up this title at www.lernerbooks.com.

Main body text set in Billy Infant Regular. Typeface provided by SparkType.

Map illustration on page 20 by Laura K. Westlund.

Library of Congress Cataloging-in-Publication Data

Names: Sanderson, Whitney, author.
Title: Meet a baby mountain lion / Whitney Sanderson.
Description: Minneapolis : Lerner Publications, [2024] | Series: Lightning bolt books - baby North American animals | Includes bibliographical references and index. | Audience: Ages 6–9 | Audience: Grades 2–3 | Summary: "Mountain lions may seem fearsome, but their babies are adorable! Readers get a fun peek at how big mountain lions are at birth, what baby mountain lions eat, and when the animals are fully grown"—Provided by publisher.
Identifiers: LCCN 2022036986 (print) | LCCN 2022036987 (ebook) | ISBN 9781728491127 (library binding) | ISBN 9781728498423 (ebook)
Subjects: LCSH: Puma—Infancy—North America—Juvenile literature.
Classification: LCC QL737.C23 S237 2024 (print) | LCC QL737.C23 (ebook) | DDC 599.75/24—dc23/eng/20220803

LC record available at https://lccn.loc.gov/2022036986
LC ebook record available at https://lccn.loc.gov/2022036987

Manufactured in the United States of America
1-53043-51061-12/6/2022

Table of Contents

Birth **4**

Learning from Mom **8**

Silent Hunter **12**

All Grown Up **16**

Habitat in Focus **20**

Fun Facts **21**

Glossary **22**

Learn More **23**

Index **24**

Birth

A mountain lion mother is ready to give birth. Her babies have been growing inside her for ninety days. The babies are called kittens or cubs.

Mountain lions have one to six cubs.

Cubs are born with their eyes closed. They weigh about 1 pound (0.5 kg), as much as a loaf of bread. They drink milk from their mother.

A cub's fur changes as it grows.

The cubs have spotted fur and blue eyes. As they grow, their fur turns brown and their eyes turn gold or green.

The mother takes care of her cubs. Mountain lion fathers live on their own.

Learning from Mom

Cubs are born in a den. When they are six weeks old, they are ready to go outside.

Mountain lions sometimes use caves as dens.

Their mother leaves them in a safe place while she hunts. She sometimes moves them to a new den.

Cubs at play

Cubs play by pouncing on one another. Playing sharpens their hunting skills. They stop drinking milk and start eating meat at around six weeks old.

Mountain lions growl, hiss, and shriek when they feel threatened. They do not roar. But they do chirp and purr.

Mountain lions sound like house cats at times!

Silent Hunter

Mountain lions most often eat deer. They will also hunt elk, rabbits, turkeys, and other animals.

Mountain lions are ambush hunters. That means they sneak up on their prey. They hunt mostly at night.

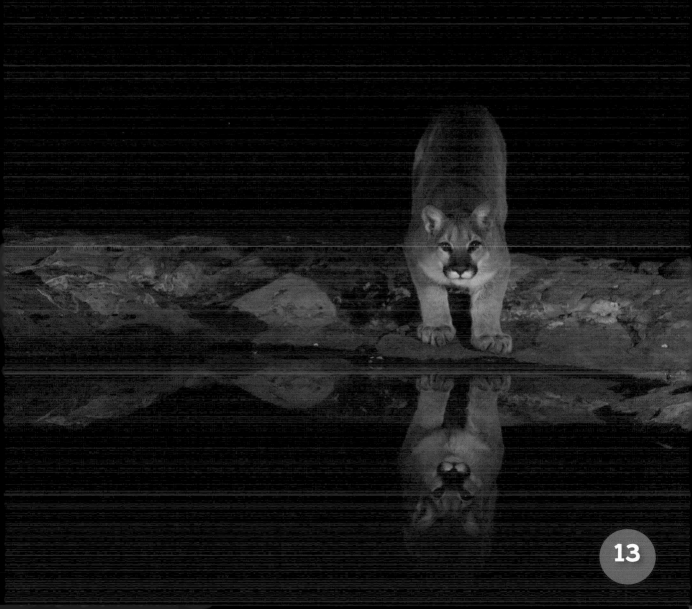

Mountain lions eat leftover food until it's gone.

A mother mountain lion shares her kill with her cubs. She does not let any meat go to waste. She covers up leftovers with leaves and dirt.

When the cubs are six months old, they weigh 35 to 45 pounds (16 to 20 kg). They practice hunting. But it can take many tries before they catch a meal!

All Grown Up

The cubs are grown by about three years old. They leave their mothers before that. A female mountain lion weighs 65 to 140 pounds (30 to 64 kg). A male can weigh up to 220 pounds (100 kg).

Other animals stay away when they smell traces of mighty mountain lions!

Mountain lion territories can cover more than 100 square miles (259 sq. km). The animal marks its territory by rubbing against trees and rocks. It may also spray urine.

Mountain lions kill a deer for food about once a week. They save energy by resting between hunts. Like all cats, they find a comfortable place to snooze.

A mountain lion at rest

Mountain lions are ready to have babies by the age of two and a half. They start the life cycle over!

Mountain Lion Life Cycle

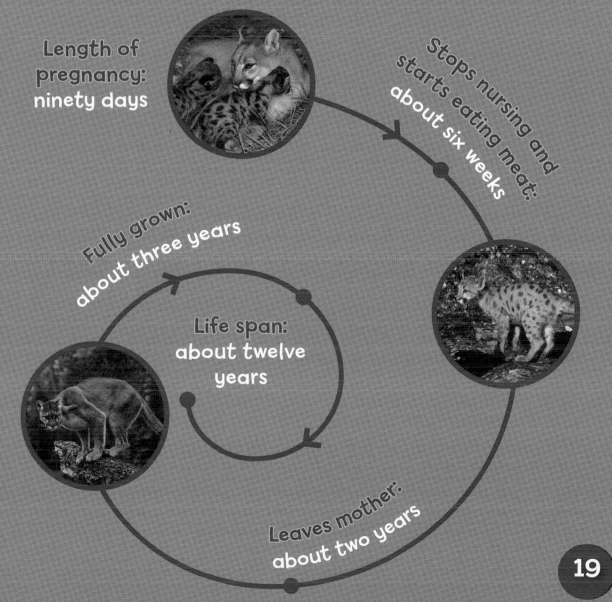

Length of pregnancy: ninety days

Stops nursing and starts eating meat: about six weeks

Fully grown: about three years

Life span: about twelve years

Leaves mother: about two years

Habitat in Focus

- Mountain lions once lived across much of North America. Then their range shrank so they no longer lived in most eastern states. But lately they've been spotted farther east.

- Mountain lions live as far north as Canada in North America. They live as far south as Chile in South America.

- Mountain lions can make their homes in mountains, deserts, forests, and swamps.

Fun Facts

- Mountain lions are known by many names, including puma, cougar, and panther.

- Mountain lions don't leave claw marks when they walk.

- A mountain lion can jump a distance of 40 feet (12 m). That's the length of a school bus!

- One type of mountain lion, the Florida panther, still lives in the eastern United States. It is endangered.

Glossary

ambush: to attack by surprise

cycle: a repeating set of events or actions

den: a sheltered area where an animal sleeps

mark: when an animal leaves signs that it was in a place

prey: an animal that another animal hunts for food

territory: the area where an animal lives or travels

Learn More

Mountain Lion Foundation: Kid's Corner
https://mountainlion.org/about-mountain-lions
/kids-corner/

Murray, Tamika M. *Meet a Baby Gray Wolf.*
Minneapolis: Lerner Publications, 2024.

National Geographic Kids: Mountain Lion
https://kids.nationalgeographic.com/animals
/mammals/facts/mountain-lion

Pincus, Meeg. *Cougar Crossing: How Hollywood's
Celebrity Cougar Helped Build a Bridge for City
Wildlife.* New York: Beach Lane Books, 2021.

San Diego Zoo Wildlife Explorers: Mountain Lion
https://sdzwildlifeexplorers.org/animals/mountain
-lion

Shaffer, Lindsay. *Mountain Lions.* Minneapolis:
Bellwether Media, 2020.

Index

den, 8-9

eyes, 5-6

fur, 6

hunting, 9-10, 12-13, 15, 18

pouncing, 10
prey, 13

territory, 17

Photo Acknowledgments

Image credits: GlobalP/Getty Images, p. 4; slowmotiongli/Getty Images, pp. 5, 19; Tambako the Jaguar/Getty Images, pp. 6, 7; Warren A Metcalf/Getty Images, pp. 8, 19; bLAZER76/ Getty Images, p. 9; Octavio Campos Salles/Alamy Stock Photo, p. 10; AYImages/Getty Images, p. 11; KenCanning/Getty Images, p. 12; MelaniWright/Getty Images, p. 13; Russell Millner/Alamy Stock Photo, p. 14; Kevin Schafer/Getty Images, p. 15; John Conrad/Getty Images, p. 16; dssimages/Getty Images, pp. 17, 19; Corney Coetzee/Getty Images, p. 18; Laura Westlund, p. 20.

Cover: Jeff Wendorff/Getty Images